When Our Mothers Become Ancestors

When Our Mothers Become Ancestors

A Survival Handbook for Love, Loss, and What Comes After

Robin E Anderson

Goddesses in the Garden Press

Chicago, Illinois

Published by Goddesses in the Garden Press
© 2026 Goddesses in the Garden, LLC

ISBN: 979-8-9944244-0-7

Printed in the United States of America

Cover Design by Robin E Anderson

This book is a work of lived experience and reflection. Names and identifying details have been changed where appropriate.

First edition

Akoma means "heart," and it is a symbol of love, goodwill, patience, faithfulness, fondness, endurance, and consistency. Though the heart shape is a universal symbol representing love, it is also an Adinkra symbol with a slightly different meaning. As an Adinkra, the heart shape represents patience and tolerance.

In Akan, "Nya akoma," literally "Get a heart" means take heart–be patient. Conversely, one who is impatient is said not to have a heart: "Onni akoma."

Being a caregiver is all about love, patience, endurance, and goodwill. I believe the Akoma is the perfect symbol for 'caregiver'.

The meaning of the symbol was taken from The Adinkra Dictionary by W. Bruce Willis.

Dedication

For my Mother,
my first home,
my first love,
my safest place,
my greatest teacher.

You taught me how to love,
how to care for others,
how to endure in spite of and because of,
and how to let go - with grace.

Your presence is larger now;
in breath, in birds, in moonlight,
in sunbeams, and in the wisdom guiding me.

♡

Acknowledgments

I give thanks for my family, who walked this journey with me in ways seen and unseen.

My sisters, my children, and all who showed up when strength was thin.

I give thanks for the caregivers, nurses, doctors, therapists, hospice workers, and angels in human form who held space with reverence and compassion.

I give thanks for friends who brought food, sat in silence, listened without fixing, and stayed long after others faded away.

I give thanks for every daughter who will see herself in these pages and know she is not alone.

And finally, I give thanks for the ancestors - especially the mothers - whose love continues beyond breath, beyond form, beyond time.

A special thank-you to my Spiritual Career Coach for lovingly guiding me through it all.

This book exists because love does not disappear — it transforms.

♥

In loving memory of my dear friend, Gwendolyn Vernita Davis (Smith), whose presence, wisdom, and grace touched my life more deeply than words can hold. This book was completed during the season of her transition. The gift of her friendship, warmth, and steady presence remain part of the circle that held me as these pages came into being. May her love continue, beyond breath and time.

Table of Contents

Prologue
• The Thing I Feared Most

Part I - The First Shifts

Chapter 1
• The First Sign

Chapter 2
• Bringing You Home

Chapter 3
• The Stroke That Changed Everything

Chapter 4
• Life Between the Storms

Chapter 5
• Letter to Mommy: Trying My Best

Chapter 6
• What Strokes Leave Behind

Chapter 7
• The Grief Before the Grief

Caregiver Guidance
• Navigating Anticipatory Grief

Part II - Becoming the Advocate

Chapter 8
• Asking for Help (and Teaching Mommy She Mattered)

Chapter 9
• Advocacy, Voice, and Honoring Wishes

Chapter 10
• When the Bottom Dropped Out

Part III - Understanding Death While Living

Chapter 11
• Understanding Death Through the Lens of Life

Chapter 12
• The Womb and the Transition

♡

Part IV - The Threshold

Chapter 13
• The Day Everything Shifted

Chapter 14
• The Last Days

Chapter 15
• Riding Out on a Moonbeam

Dear Mommy
• Walking You to the Door

Chapter 16
• The Last Acts of Love

Chapter 17
• The Longest Walk

Part V - The World After

Chapter 18
• When the World Reaches Out

Chapter 19
• The Sign

Reflection
• The Meaning of Hummingbirds

• The Swallowtail Miracle
(On Transformation, Energy, and Continuity)

Chapter 20
• The Next Day

Letters to Mommy

• Trying My Best
• Walking You to the Door
• Three Years Later

Prologue

The Morning After

Dear Mommy,

The thing I feared most has happened.

I woke up this morning and the world felt wrong—tilted, unfamiliar, too quiet.
There was no reason to reach for my phone. No "Good morning, Mommy."
No familiar smile echoing through the line.
No voice anchoring me to the start of the day.

I don't know what to do – how to live, how to breathe – without you.
You have known what it is to live without me, but I have never known life without you. I have never taken a breath that wasn't somehow attached to yours.

We always joked that if you ever tried to die, I'd just bring you right back.

You'd get to the pearly gates, greet St. Peter, maybe even slip one foot inside – and in the blink of an eye, you'd be back in the kitchen, making coffee for us like nothing happened.

You'd laugh that soft, knowing laugh and say,
"Please, Robin... just let me go. When it's time, let me go."

I never thought I'd be able to.
I never thought my arms, my heart, my spirit would have the strength to do something so impossible.

But in the end, Mommy... I did.
It happened.

And I let you go.

I held you—my mother, my first home, my truest companion—as you took your last breath. I felt the exact moment your soul loosened itself from your body. I felt the air change, the energy shift, the strange and holy stillness that came after.

And now, I don't know how to breathe.

People say you see your life flash before your eyes when you die.
When you left, my life flashed before mine.

Every morning phone call.
Every laugh.
Every lesson.
Every time your hand steadied me.
Every time your presence reminded me that even when the world
was rough, I had a place to land.

Mommy, I always knew this day would come.
But I never expected it to arrive.
Not like this.
Not in my arms.
Not in the quiet way death can slip into a room and rearrange
everything.

What am I supposed to do tomorrow?

xoxoxo,
Robin

Part I ~ The First Shifts

I used to begin each day the same way: calling my mother.
It wasn't just a habit—it was a rhythm, the steady heartbeat
that shaped my mornings. "Good morning, Mommy" was
more than a greeting. It was a grounding. A blessing. A ritual
that aligned my spirit before the rest of the world had a chance
to touch it.

My mother and I were close. Close.
The kind of close people don't always understand, the kind
that makes them smile knowingly or say things like, "Y'all are
the same person."
My sister says that all the time.

I don't agree - we were alike, yes, but also beautifully different.
But make no mistake: I am my mother's daughter.
Her humor, her fire, her softness, her stubbornness, her grace -
they live in me like echoes and roots.

Now, everywhere I look, I see her.
Her reflection where mine should be.
Her face in every mirror, every windowpane catching the
morning light.
Her presence in every photograph that once felt like memory,
but now feels like oxygen.

She lives through me.
And yet, I am still learning how to live without her.

This is the story of those final days - our final days.
Of caregiving and love, of fear and surrender, of the sacredness
that can rise even in the shadow of death.
It is the story of how a daughter let her mother go, and how a
mother stayed anyway - in the breath, in the bone, in the quiet
places the living don't always know how to look.

And it begins here, in the space between one last breath and my
next one.

Chapter One

The First Sign

The first sign was small - so small it almost slipped past me.
But intuition has a way of whispering before anything shouts.

That morning, I called Mommy the way I always did.
It was ritual, muscle memory, the way my spirit aligned itself
before I stepped into the day. I was on my way to a full-day
workshop, the kind that would take all of my focus, and I needed
my sunshine before I walked in.

"Are you eating?" I asked her.
Something in her voice sounded... off.
Thick. Muffled. Like there was something in her mouth.

"No, I'm not eating," she said.

"Are you okay?"
She said she was fine - firmly enough that I paused, but softly
enough that I didn't quite believe her.

"I'm coming over," I told her.

"No, no, no - go to your class. I'm fine."
She always hated to be an inconvenience, even to the people
who loved her most.

Still uneasy, I called my sister.
She lived 750 miles away but distance never stopped her from
jumping into action. She checked in with Mommy and called
me back with what she thought was reassurance:
"She sounds okay."

So I went to my session.

But on the drive, that uneasy feeling tugged at me again.
I started calling her closest friends - women who had known
her for decades, women who called her sister, women who
promised to swing by and check on her right away.

They assured me they would.
My sister was on top of it.
I tried to focus, tried to quiet the knot in my stomach.

♡

Hours later, when I checked in to see who had stopped by, I learned the truth:

No one had gone.

My heart sank.

I had been sitting in a workshop trying to learn, trying to be present, while my mother sat alone - waiting, denying, trying to be "fine" the way mothers do even when they aren't.

I didn't hesitate.
I gathered my things and left. Fast.
Six hours had passed. Six hours too many.

When I arrived at her condo, one friend - one who had promised to be there hours earlier - had shown up maybe half an hour before me.

She greeted me casually, almost dismissively, as though everything was normal, as though time, for me, hadn't stretched into worry and fear.

"She's fine," the friend insisted.

But I could feel it, something was not fine. Something had shifted in the invisible space between who my mother had been and who she was becoming.

"I want her outside," I said, my voice steady in a way that only comes from fear. "Bring her to my car."

I could feel her blinking and looking at my mother, surprised.
But I wasn't asking.
I was instructing.

Mommy was going home with me.

Chapter Two

Bringing You Home

The Stroke

Once we arrived at my house, everything in me went into caregiver mode.

I made her some tea, warm and herbal - the kind she always said "hit the spot" - and I tucked her into the guest (her) bed like she was the child and I was the mother.

She looked fine.

But something in her spirit wasn't sitting right with me. Her eyes were a little dull, her movements a little delayed. Her "I'm fine" didn't ring true - not to a daughter who knew every version of her mother.

"Mommy, maybe we should go to the emergency room," I said gently.

She gave me that look.
That absolutely not look.

And of course she wasn't going to go.

Not that day. Not on her terms.

So I let the night hold us both.

The next day I pampered her - my version of care, love, and vigilance all rolled into one.

I made her a light breakfast and brought it to her in bed.

Propped her pillows.

Turned on her beloved Bears game.

Watched her with the eyes of someone who knew something was coming but couldn't yet name it.

She seemed... normal.

Not perfect, not fully herself, but normal enough that I tried to let the worry loosen its grip on my chest.

We had a sweet night.

We laughed, ate our favorite snacks, teased each other the way we always did. For a moment, life felt like it always had - Mommy and me, in our rhythm, in our bubble, just us.

The next morning, she came downstairs for breakfast.

She sat at the table, picked up her fork, and... paused.

♡

Her hand hovered awkwardly.
She pushed her food around, trying to gather it, but her
movements were slow, disorganized, unsure.

The day before, the food had been all finger foods - easy, familiar,
something she could pick up instinctively. Today was different.
Today required coordination her body could no longer muster.

I watched her in silence for a few seconds that felt like a lifetime.

Then I said, "Mommy, we're going to the ER. You need medical
attention."

She refused.

Of course she refused.
My mother was nothing if not strong willed - a trait I definitely
inherited.

So I called her doctor.
I told him everything I was seeing, every strange moment, every
hesitation in her movements.

He didn't hesitate.

"Take her to the emergency room immediately," he said. "It sounds like she's had a stroke."

I told Mommy. She shook her head again.
"No."

I put the phone back to my ear.
"Doctor," I said, "she refuses. Apparently, she'd rather go to the morgue.

Mommy glared at me.
Then she got her coat.

My mother had had a stroke on Saturday morning in the twilight hours, long before either of us understood what was happening. It was now Monday morning.

We rushed to the hospital where her doctor practiced, and what followed was seven long days - seven days of fear and hope, tests and waiting, tiny improvements and new concerns.

Seven days where I barely left her side.
Where sleeping in chairs became normal.
Where my world became hospital hallways, medical monitors, whispered prayers, and the quiet between moments.

15

It was the beginning of many hospital and rehab stays.
And from that moment on, I was with her - day and night, every step of the journey, holding together whatever parts of her life the stroke tried to take.

It was the start of the slow, sacred path toward her transition.

LETTER TO MY FUTURE SELF
(or to anyone caregiving)

Dear Robin,

One day you will look back at this moment - the fear, the confusion, the weight of not knowing - and you will see the strength you couldn't see then.

You didn't know what was happening.
You didn't know what was coming.
All you knew was that something in your mother's spirit had shifted, and you answered that shift with love.

You did not fail her.
You did not miss the signs.
You traced them - slowly, painfully, intuitively - until they revealed themselves.

She didn't want you to worry.
She didn't want to be a burden.

Even in her weakening, she was your mother, still trying to protect you.

But you protected her, too.
You listened when her words said, "I'm fine," and her body whispered, "I'm not."

You showed up.
You acted.
You loved her through the unknown.

This is what daughters do
when they become the mother
to the woman who once mothered them.

You did it beautifully.

And when you read this later - years from now - may you remember that love guided every step, even the steps you questioned.

With tenderness,
Me (or You)

What to Do When Something Feels "Off"

When caring for someone you love - especially a parent - your intuition becomes a medical instrument. You may not know the diagnosis, but you will feel the first shift.

Here are gentle instructions for anyone facing what I faced:

1. Trust your intuition, even when they insist they're fine.

Mothers, fathers, elders - they often hide discomfort to "protect" us.
A subtle change in voice, coordination, appetite, or mood is enough to warrant attention.

2. Don't wait for proof. Respond to the feeling.

If something feels wrong, act.
Call. Ask questions. Observe.
You don't need certainty to seek help.

3. Mobilize your circle early.

Ask friends, family, neighbors to check in.
And check that they actually do.

Dependable help is vital.
Accountability is too.

4. Document changes.

Even tiny ones.
Doctors rely on what you notice.

5. Don't be afraid to push back.

Medical professionals, friends, even the loved one themselves may dismiss your concern.
Advocate anyway.

6. If they won't go to the ER, call their doctor.

Doctors can persuade in ways family sometimes cannot.
If the doctor says go - go.

7. You may have to become "the parent" for a moment.

It will feel strange.
It may feel disrespectful.
But it is an act of profound love.

8. You are not overreacting. You are protecting.

Your fear is not weakness.
Your vigilance is vital care.

9. Prepare for the long journey, but take it one day at a time.

Hospital stays. Rehab. Follow-up care.

Allow yourself to learn as you go.
No one knows how to do this until they have to.

10. You are not alone.

Even when it feels like you are.
There is a community of caregivers navigating the same uncertain path, learning to hold their loved ones while holding themselves.

Chapter Three

The Stroke That Changed Everything

Fight to Recover

Mommy was born on the cusp of Aries and Taurus - fire and earth, stubbornness and spark, determination and sheer will braided into one woman.
So you can imagine how ready she was to go home as quickly as possible.

From the moment she was coherent enough, she answered every question the nurses and doctors threw at her:

"What day is it?"
"Who's the president?"
"Do you know where you are?"

She spoke with clarity, confidence, and that little hint of attitude that meant, I'm getting out of here soon, don't play with me.

♡

She pushed through every therapy exercise. If they told her to lift her arm ten times, she'd try to do twelve. When they said rest, she'd say, "I can do one more."

That was Mommy.
Our Aries–Taurus hybrid warrior.

Meanwhile, I created a sanctuary in that hospital room.

Every night, I did her hair - gentle strokes, careful parts - because dignity lives in the details. I moisturized her skin, massaged her hands, kept our most powerful crystals and oils placed around the room like an invisible circle of protection.

The nurses would come in and say, "It smells like a spa in here."

Good.
Healing should.

And of course, Coco Chanel was there - our faithful little Shorkie, certified Emotional Support Animal with the official paperwork to prove it. She was small enough to tuck under my arm, alert enough to sense every shift in Mommy's mood, and sweet enough that even the toughest nurse would soften in her presence.

♡

Some days, staff members would poke their heads in and whisper,
"Can we sit in here for a minute? It's peaceful."

We welcomed them all.
Even in crisis, Mommy remained a source of calm for other people.
That was her quiet magic.

Every morning, I slipped out early - before the sun fully rose - to take Coco Chanel for her walk. Then I'd grab our familiar comforts: coffee, croissants, oatmeal. I tried to recreate our normal morning rhythm as best as I could in a room full of beeping machines and unfamiliar footsteps.

And it worked.
She was recovering.
Truly recovering.

By the time she was discharged, everyone was cheering her on. Her doctor said she was on her way to a full return. She was strong, moving well, remembering well - our mother was coming back to us.

Six months later, she had another stroke.

This time it affected the other side of her brain.

It was a cruel symmetry - one stroke on each side, bookending the progress she had fought so hard to make.

This second stroke taught me something I now share with every caregiver I meet.

Caregiver Note: The Importance of a "Go Bag"

When a medical emergency strikes, you don't think clearly.

You scramble.

You forget things.

You panic.

You go into autopilot - and autopilot is rarely organized.

So let me say this plainly:

Every caregiver needs a "**go bag**."

Keep it packed. Keep it by the door. Update it often.

What to include:

- Copies of all medical records
- A complete list of medications
- Insurance cards
- Comfort items (socks, lotion, lip balm, a soft blanket)
- A notebook and pen
- Snacks and water bottle
- A phone charger
- Advance directives, if available
- A spare set of clothes for both of you

♡

- Any essential devices (glasses, hearing aids, mobility aids)
- YOUR medication/supplements/vitamins
- Toiletries
- Warm socks and perhaps a sweater or shawl, those hospital rooms are cold
- Comfy shoes - for you

Any special item they want - Mommy used sensitive toothpaste, it was always in the bag.

And yes, even though hospitals often say, "Don't bring their medications," you'd be shocked how often they don't have what's needed right away, or how long it can take for pharmacy orders to come through.

Having your loved one's medication list in your hand - and the physical medications in a separate, clearly labeled bag - can save precious time and prevent serious mistakes.

A "**go bag**" is not a luxury.
It is a lifeline.

Chapter Four

Life Between the Storms

Between the first and second stroke,
we lived life.

After the first stroke, Mommy had a cane - naturally it was cute,
stylish, and the kind of cane you'd expect an Aries/Taurus DST
diva to carry. Everywhere we went, someone complimented it.
She'd smile a little, pretend she didn't notice, and then make sure I
heard the compliment twice.

We also had a transport wheelchair.
That chair changed everything.

It took some convincing to get her to use it - my mother was
independent to the bone. But once she surrendered to the
convenience, the comfort, the ease... she didn't look back. It
became our chariot, our little freedom mobile.

And once her medical team cleared her?

We were gone.

Movies.

Dinners.

Plays.

Shopping sprees.

Walks outside just to feel the sun on her face.

We even flew to Texas for my middle son's wedding - an entire adventure fueled by determination, excitement, and the kind of energy only a recovering queen could radiate.

Mommy and I were always going somewhere together.

But now?

Now I moved with a sense of urgency.

I wanted more memories.

I wanted laughter.

I wanted moments stamped onto the pages of time.

And I sensed she did too.

We didn't say it out loud, but both of us knew:
life had shifted.

Time felt different now.
More precious.
More fragile.
More immediate.

We lived deeply in those six months.
And then - like the first one - stroke number two crept in quietly,
disguised as an ordinary morning.

My Dad, who lives 778 miles away and loves to beat me to the
"Good morning" call, reached Mommy first that day. He phoned
me immediately after speaking to her.

"Miss Robin, she's not able to walk," he said, his voice tight.

He told me she said she'd rolled off her bed and crawled to a chair
to help herself stand.

Crawled.

My heart dropped, and I rushed out the door.

And before anyone wonders why she wasn't living with me, let me make something clear:

You didn't know my mother.

She was wildly independent - fiercely so.
She had never depended on anyone for anything, and she wasn't about to start now.

That's why, on every trip to the ER, I had her chanting:
"I matter."
Over and over, until she believed it.
Eventually... she did.

When I arrived, she was walking, standing, talking - feigning ignorance as if nothing had ever happened. I made her a seven-minute egg exactly the way she liked them. After she went to lie down, I peeked in on her.

And that's when I saw it:
the side of her face had begun to slide.

The quiet, unmistakable signature of a stroke.

I called 911.

♡

I grabbed our go bag and ran to my car with tears in my eyes.

It was the height of Covid.
A time when hospitals were fortresses - no visitors, no exceptions, no comfort.

I followed the ambulance and rushed through the hospital doors, only to be stopped by security.

"No visitors allowed in the ER."

I panicked.

I begged.
I pleaded.
I cried.

"My mother is alone. She has no phone, no glasses, she's not talking, she has no way to advocate for herself. She needs me."

They still said no.

I called her doctor. His nurse tried to calm me.

"They'll arrest you if you try to go in," she warned.

"I'm going to jail then," I said without hesitation.

She shared her own pain - her 90-year-old father had been admitted just days before, and even as an employee, she wasn't allowed inside.

"That's unfortunate, my mommy is different," I countered.

"He has dementia," she whispered.

I paused.

Even though I felt her heartbreak, I couldn't surrender mine.

She told me something that finally reached through the panic:

"If you're in jail, what happens to her then?"

She won (she'd really won with the dementia comment). I asked her, "what can I do?'

She encouraged me to call the ER desk and speak to Mommy's nurse, which I did.
A kind nurse came outside right away, retrieved Mommy's belongings, and I was able to FaceTime her within minutes.

There she was.
My mother.

Talking.
Smiling.
Brave in the face of fear.

I prayed.
I thanked The Most High (TMH).
I called my sister back - she arrived that same night.

I sat outside the hospital for four hours, waiting to speak to my mother's doctor.
She stayed another seven days.

By the time they transferred her to rehab, restrictions had eased slightly:
one visitor
the same visitor
for the entire stay.

My sister insisted that I go.

Mommy's room was on the first floor, so she and my sister could see each other through the window—pressing hands to opposite sides of glass, the pandemic version of holding on.

They even let me bring Coco Chanel to see her each night. Tucked in her carrier, she'd poke her little head out and look at Mommy like, I'm here. We're here.

Every morning, I arrived early with:

-     her breakfast of choice
-     a thermos of hot coffee
-     fresh flowers for her room

The entire staff fell in love with her—how could they not?

She was an 86 year old elegant lady, strong as a bull, stubborn as a ram, grounded as Mother Earth, and the soft, gentle mother who had loved us fiercely all our lives.

We were simply grateful she'd survived, without any obvious constraints, again.

♡

Letter to Mommy: Trying My Best

Dear Mommy,

I'm trying to be brave.
I'm trying to be thorough.
I'm trying to be the woman you raised me to be.

But I'm scared.

When the team of doctors come in, I take notes - every detail,
every instruction, every possibility hidden between their words.
I ask the questions I know you would want asked, the ones you
would insist on if your voice were strong enough in this
moment.

The hospital is hectic.
Everyone is exhausted.
They're short-staffed because of covid, and the whole system
feels stretched thin.

So I help.
I do what I can.

I ask for what you need, and I make sure they know:
if there's something I can't handle, I will call them.

They still check in periodically, but it feels like we're a team - me,
you, Coco Chanel, the handful of nurses who whisper 'thanks'
when they step out of your room. They appreciate that I'm here,
that I'm steady, that I'm trying to hold things together.

But Mommy...
I'm doing my best.
And I pray it's enough.

xoxoxo
Robin

♡

Caregiver Reflection: The Night Someone Took Care of Me

Mommy was a Southern Belle, raised by a Southern Belle.
Modest. Demure. Gentle. Genteel.
Even in a hospital bed, she carried herself with the quiet dignity
of a woman taught to move through life with grace.

So I made it my responsibility to protect that dignity,
to keep her comfortable, discreet, moisturized, and cared for,
even when the world around us felt chaotic and unkind.

One night, a lovely nurse stepped into the room with a warmth
in her eyes that stopped me in my tracks.

"I heard about you," she said.

My brows lifted.
"Oh really? What'd you hear?"

She chuckled. "Nothing bad. But tonight, you are going to get
some sleep. You need it, and you will not drop from exhaustion
on my watch."

I didn't realize how much I needed someone to say that; to look
at me and see past the strength, past the composure, past the
determined daughter holding everything together.

It felt almost foreign to be cared for
after so many days and nights of caretaking.

But Covid had stretched the staff thin, and despite her best
efforts, we didn't see much of her that night.
Her effort, though, was a balm.
A reminder that compassion still existed,
even in a world suffocating under crisis.

Through it all -

the hospital stays,
the ER visits,
the rehab centers,
the countless appointments -
we somehow managed to avoid contracting Covid.

A quiet miracle.
One of the many ways God held us through that season.

♡

Chapter Five

What Strokes Leave Behind

No one prepares you for what happens after the hospital releases your loved one.

The world celebrates survival.

Cards come in, prayers rise up, people say, "Thank God she made it."

But what they don't tell you is this:

Strokes don't only damage the body.

They rearrange the mind.

They rewrite behavior.

They alter rhythms you've known your whole life.

And sometimes... they take the person you knew and return a different version of them, one you must learn to love in new ways.

♡

Mommy had always been sharp.

Quick-witted.

Observant.

A woman who could tell you where something was stored even if she hadn't opened the drawer in ten years.

So when things began to shift, I noticed.

♡

The Emotional Echo of Hospital Life

Long-term and frequent hospitalization wears on a person.
For someone modest and dignified like Mommy, being poked,
prodded, monitored, and watched around the clock was more
than uncomfortable - it was humiliating at times, even with the
best staff.

Hospital rooms blur time.
Days lose their edges.
Sleeping through noise becomes impossible.
Pain, fear, and disorientation settle in.

Repeated admissions created a cycle:
- Confusion
- Frustration
- Emotional exhaustion
- Withdrawal
- Moments of agitation
- Moments of intense vulnerability

She was strong, but hospitals chip away at even the strongest
spirits.

And strokes?

♡

They multiply the effect.

Sundowning: When Night Changes Everything

It started subtly - a little restlessness, a little anxiety as the sun set.

Then, gradually, evenings became different.

Sundowning is common after strokes and during early cognitive decline:

- Confusion increases as it gets dark.
- Anxiety heightens.
- Mood shifts rapidly.
- Shadows or dim light make the brain misinterpret the environment.
- The person may feel unsafe, lost, or suspicious.

With Mommy, evenings could be soft or turbulent; we never knew which version the night would bring.

Some nights she was chatty, reflective, nostalgic.
Other nights she became disoriented, repeating questions, or worrying about things she couldn't articulate.

And my job, as always, was to anchor her.

To adjust the lights, soften the room, play her favorite shows or music, hold her hand, rub her back, remind her over and over:

"You're safe.
I'm here, we're here.
You're not alone."

♡

Early Signs of Dementia: The Ones No One Warns You About

People think dementia begins with forgetting names or getting disoriented.
But the earliest signs are often emotional and behavioral - and they can be shocking.

Here are the ones we encountered:

1. Accusations of Stealing

This is one of the most painful symptoms for families.

When a loved one misplaces something, the brain can no longer retrace steps logically.
Instead of thinking, "I must've put it somewhere," the mind jumps to:

"Someone took it from me."

It feels personal - like a betrayal.
But it's not.
It is the brain trying to make sense of gaps in memory.

2. Out-of-Place Statements

Mommy would say things that didn't fit the moment or the environment:

- talking about people who weren't there
- recalling events that didn't happen
- describing places that didn't exist
- insisting something urgent was happening when it wasn't

These moments were startling... and heartbreaking.

The woman who raised me on logic, elegance, and common sense was suddenly making statements that didn't belong anywhere in reality.

3. Emotional Misfires

Sudden anger.
Startling sadness.
Childlike fear.
Moments of agitation with no obvious cause.

Not because she wanted to be difficult.
But because her brain was misfiring - sending signals out of order, out of context, out of rhythm.

4. Difficulty Processing New Information

Even minor changes became overwhelming:

- a new nurse
- a different room
- moving furniture
- appointments
- unfamiliar routines

Her mind preferred the familiar, the predictable, the known.

Learning to Respond, Not React

I had to learn - slowly, painfully - that logic no longer worked.
That correcting her made things worse.
That arguing with confusion only deepened it.

Instead, I learned to:
- validate her feelings
- redirect gently
- soothe instead of explain
- simplify choices
- offer reassurance repeatedly
- remain calm even when she wasn't

And always...
always...
honor her dignity.

Mommy was still Mommy.
Even when her mind slipped into places from which she could not fully return.

My job was not to pull her back.

It was to meet her where she was, walk with her there, and bring softness into whatever space her brain created.

The Cleverness of My Mother

There's something people don't tell you about dementia -
especially in the early stages:

Smart people hide it.
Really, really well.

My mommy was brilliant.
Sharp.
Socially aware.
Emotionally intelligent.
A woman who could read a room before she stepped into it.
So when her mind began to slip in small places, she didn't panic.

She adapted.

If she said something that didn't make sense and I gently asked,
"Mommy, what did you say?"
she would wave her hand and reply,

"Never mind."

Quick.
Dismissive.

Smooth.

And she would not repeat it.

She knew exactly how to cover the gaps.
She picked up on my cues instantly - the slight tilt of my head, the pause in my breath, the way I tried to hide concern behind a smile.

She sensed it all.

And because she sensed me,
she adjusted.

That was her brilliance.
Her survival instinct.
Her pride.
Her Southern Belle dignity wrapped around a Taurus spine of steel.

She refused to let the world see her falter.

The Accusations, the Anger, and the Humor That Saved Me

But hiding has limits.

As the strokes took more from her - tiny pieces at a time - the early signs of cognitive decline became harder to mask.

The confusion.
The misplaced items.
The accusations.

"Who took my purse?"
"Somebody came in here."
"What did you two do with my things?"

If I had taken it personally,
if I had tried to argue or reason,
it would have shattered me.

So instead...

I laughed.

Not to mock.
Not to dismiss.

But to survive.

I laughed because the alternative was collapsing.
I laughed because the madness of it all would have drowned me
if I didn't.
I laughed because sometimes humor is the only thing standing
between you and the heartbreak of watching your mother
change in ways she never wanted you to see.

And sometimes -

she laughed with me.

She'd roll her eyes,
or pretend she didn't understand what was funny,
or brush me off with her hand the way only she could.

But the laughter opened the door.
It softened the sharp edges.
It reminded us both that underneath everything -
beneath the confusion and the fear and the shifting brain
chemistry -
we still knew each other.
We were still us.

Laughter held the pieces together when the truth threatened to break them apart.

The Cleverness That Stayed Until the End

Even as the decline progressed,
my mother remained clever.

She learned how to hide what she couldn't fix.
She adjusted when she sensed concern.
She pretended when reality slipped.
She protected me from the full weight of what she was
experiencing.

That was her love.
Her legacy.
Her way of mothering even while I mothered her.

And I cannot tell you how many times her quick wit,
her pride,
her stubborn charm,
and her instinct to "keep it together"
made me laugh in the middle of some of the hardest nights of my
life.

She was slipping - yes.
But she never stopped being her.

Smart.

Perceptive.

Slick.

Sassy when she felt it.

A little magician with her mind, rearranging reality just enough to hold onto dignity.

My mommy was clever until the end.

And I loved her for it.

The Jewelry Box Incident

One day in particular stands out so clearly that I can still feel the
energy of it.

I went to Mommy's house - my sister had abandoned her life in
Alabama and had been staying with her for a while now - and I
think we were supposed to run errands, maybe go get groceries or
something simple like that.

But the moment I walked in, the atmosphere felt... off.
Both of them were looking strange, jittery even.

My sister pulled me aside and said,
"We've been looking for a specific box of jewelry all night."

All night?

I asked a few questions, trying to get the lay of the land, and then
decided to join the hunt. Mommy insisted the box had been under
her bed, so I got down on my hands and knees, determined to
show them they must have overlooked it.

Surely, I thought, it was right there.

But as I started pulling things out from under the bed, I caught a glimpse of my mother's face.

And whew.

The look she gave me was pure suspicion - skepticism so heavy it could've been bottled and sold.
Her eyes were saying:

"Look at her, pretending to look for what she already stole."

The thought hit me so hard I almost choked.

The audacity of it.
The comedy of it.

The absurdity of me - her daughter - being accused of running a sophisticated jewelry heist in my spare time.

I laughed so hard I had to sit back on my heels.

It was either laugh or get my feelings hurt... and laughter won by a mile.

♡

"Mommy," I said, trying to breathe through the giggles,
"why would I steal from you? If I wanted something you had,
I'd just ask for it!"

She didn't answer.
Didn't blink.
Just kept looking at me like she was watching the lead suspect
in an unsolved mystery.

At that point, I grabbed my bag, said "Alright, y'all got it," and
got the heck out of there.
I left them to continue their treasure hunt slash investigation
without me.

And hindsight?
Oh, hindsight is the clearest teacher of all.

Now I can look back and see the signs - little moments, little
accusations, little lapses in logic - that I chalked up to aging,
stress, or stubbornness.

But now I know better.

What I thought were quirks were early symptoms.

What I thought were personality shifts were neurological changes.

♡

What I thought was sass, was confusion wrapped in dignity.

She wasn't accusing me to hurt me.
She was trying to make sense of a world her mind was slowly rearranging without her permission.

And me?

I had to laugh to keep from falling apart.

Chapter Six

The Grief Before the Grief

People ask me about my grieving.
The truth is, I'd been grieving the loss of my mommy for years
before her transition.

When a parent begins to show decline, it doesn't start the day you
notice it.
It starts quietly, slowly, invisibly - years before any doctor uses
words like dementia or cognitive impairment or decline.

But you don't recognize it at first.
Because it creeps in like fog.
Soft.
Silent.
Gradual.

One day you wake up and find yourself saying,
"I don't know who this person is."

And you don't.
Not fully.

Because there's an imposter living inside your parent's familiar body.

Their face is the same.
Their voice is the same.
Their mannerisms are familiar.

But something has shifted.
Someone else is calling the shots from inside their avatar.

All those unwelcomed behaviors you're unfamiliar with:
the accusations,
the sharp words,
the irrational actions,
the out-of-place statements -
they represent the loss of the person you once knew.

People ask:

"How could my father say such mean things to me?"
He wouldn't.

"How could my mother think I'd steal from her?"
She doesn't.

"How could my parent throw a food tray at my face?"
They didn't.

The imposter did.
The invader.
The neurological glitch.
The clinical stranger borrowing your loved one's body.

It can feel like The Invasion of the Body Snatchers in real life.
It is terrifying.
It is heartbreaking.
It is disorienting.

But the sooner you accept this truth,
the better off you'll be:

Your parent is not doing these things,
the illness is.

Your loved one might not remember any of it.
Or they may remember and carry deep, overwhelming guilt.
Either way, it is up to you - the caregiver, the child, the witness -
to hold perspective.

To remember who they were
beneath who they are becoming.

To know your mother, father, grandparent would never behave this way intentionally.

Try not to dwell on the hurt.
Try not to hold them accountable for things they cannot control.
In the grand scheme of things, it is not the most important part of the journey.

Extend them grace.
They need it now more than ever.

And extend yourself the same.
Because loving someone through decline is not natural.
It stretches the heart in ways it wasn't designed to stretch without support.

I highly, highly recommend getting professional help - therapy, grief counseling, caregiver support - during this time.

I could not have made it otherwise.

This is the grief before the grief.
The mourning that happens while they're still alive.
The quiet, unspoken heartbreak that caregivers rarely talk about.

But it is real.

And it deserves a name, a space, a voice, a caretaker.

I'm grateful that Mommy never slipped into a dementia diagnosis, but I could see it trying to seep through.

Part II ~ Becoming the Advocate

Chapter Seven

Asking for Help (and Teaching Mommy She Mattered)

During this period, I was still taking my courses and had another important full-day session ahead of me. Missing it wasn't an option.

But leaving Mommy alone wasn't an option either.

So I did what so many caregivers struggle to do:

I asked for help.

I enlisted family members and friends early.
I created time slots and let people choose what they could cover.

Some covered an hour.
Some covered two.
One person even did a split shift - left to handle something, then came back later to finish the time they promised.

And because my mother was so kind, so warm, so deeply loved, no one minded helping.

People were honored to sit with her.

Their "yes" came easily.

She, on the other hand, was mad as the hatter.

Mommy never asked anyone for help.
She didn't know how.
Her independence wasn't solely a personality trait - it was a trauma
response we eventually healed before she transitioned.
But at that time, she was furious with me.

"Mommy," I asked gently,
"What's your mantra? Can you say it for me?"

She sighed, rolled her eyes a little, but did it:

"I matter.
I matter.
I matter."

We repeated it until she softened.

One of her most devoted neighbors - a dear friend of mine -
volunteered to cover the last three hours.
But Mommy tried to trick her into leaving.

She was still angry with me for organizing help and thought the shift was "too much" for anyone.

She had forgotten her own worth.
Forgotten that she mattered enough for people to show up.

Later, she admitted to me that she told her neighbor,
"I'm going to go to bed now so you can leave."

But my shero looked her right in the face and said,
"That's fine. You go on to bed. I'm staying to fulfill my time commitment."

Talk about integrity.

Mommy ended up staying awake with her anyway.
She wasn't planning to sleep - she just didn't want to be a burden.
By the end of the shift, she said she really enjoyed her neighbor's company.

I reminded Mommy gently that the sitters weren't just for safety; they were necessary because she was so good at hiding her symptoms.

I couldn't trust her to tell me the truth about her condition.

And there was no way I could attend my class otherwise.

Asking for help was the only way forward.

And I am forever, deeply grateful
for every single person
who walked alongside us during that journey.

Their care made my caregiving possible.
Their presence made the impossible doable.
Their love held us both.

Chapter Eight

Advocacy, Voice & Honoring Their Wishes

Caring for someone you love - especially a parent - means stepping into a world where emotions, medical decisions, instincts, and dignity all collide. What I learned walking beside my mother is this:

Advocacy is not optional.
It is sacred.
It is necessary.
It is love in action.

These are the truths I want others to know:

1. Listen to your loved one first. Always.

Doctors, nurses, friends, and even well-meaning family members will have opinions—sometimes strong ones. But your loved one's voice is the compass.

Even when they are confused...
Even when they are afraid...
Even when they insist, "I'm fine," when they are clearly not...

Their wishes matter.
Their autonomy matters.
Their right to speak for themselves matters - even in moments when others assume they cannot.

Listen for what they say.
Listen beneath what they say.
Let their energy guide your next step.

2. Insist that medical staff speak to them, not around them.

Too often, especially with elders, medical professionals direct questions to the caregiver instead of the patient. Sometimes it's habit. Sometimes it's assumption. Sometimes it's unconscious ageism.

When this happens, gently interrupt.

Say:
"Please speak to her first. I'm here for support, but she can answer for herself."

It preserves their dignity.
It encourages engagement.
It helps the medical team see them as a whole human, not a chart or condition.

And when your loved one cannot respond clearly, the staff will already be in the posture of treating them with respect.

3. Trust your intuition more than the surface-level answers.

You know them.
You know their habits, their voice, their rhythms, their spark.

If something feels off - even if they claim they're fine - listen to that feeling.
You are not being dramatic.
You are not imagining it.
The body whispers before it screams.

Let your intuition be the early warning system.

4. Advocate without apology.

You may be labeled "pushy."

You may be dismissed.
You may be told you're overreacting.
Advocate anyway.

Ask the questions.

Request the tests.
Call the doctor back.
Follow up with the nurse's station.
Ask for clarity.
Ask again if something doesn't make sense.

This is not confrontation.
This is protection.

Your loved one deserves a voice.
If theirs falters, yours becomes the echo.

5. Honor their independence, even as you step into leadership.

This is one of the hardest balancing acts:

Respecting their autonomy, while stepping in to keep them safe.

It requires tenderness, timing, and deep empathy.

Say things like:

- "I want to make sure you're heard."
- "Let's decide this together."
- "Your voice matters. I'm here to support you, not take over."

Advocacy is not about control.
It's about alignment.
Working with them, not instead of, or against them.

6. Preparation is empowerment.

Know their medications.
Know their doctors.
Know their insurance.
Know their baseline.*
Know how they prefer to make decisions.
Know what "quality of life" means to them, not just to you.

When the moment comes - and it always comes - you won't be scrambling.
You'll be grounded, steady, present.

7. Your advocacy creates safety in frightening moments.

When my mother could not walk, when her speech faltered, when Covid barriers locked us out, when medical systems made assumptions, she knew one thing with absolute certainty:

Her daughter would not abandon her voice.

That knowing carries more healing than any medication.

Advocacy is protection.
Advocacy is dignity.
Advocacy is love.

And when the time comes to let them go, you will know in your heart:

You honored who they were and what mattered to them.

*Baseline means their usual, functional indicators - not textbook averages.
These may include:
Blood pressure (their normal, not "ideal")
Heart rate
A1C or blood sugar trends

PSA levels

Oxygen saturation

Weight fluctuations

Kidney function numbers

Appetite patterns

Sleep habits

Mobility and balance

Speech clarity and cognitive behavior

You know what's normal for your loved one; medical 'normal' is not always personal normal.

When something suddenly changes, or seems off - even if it's in the 'okay' range, say something.

You are not overreacting; you are paying attention. Your observation can be the difference between intervention and crisis.

You know your loved one best. Rely on that; trust that.

Thankfully, Mommy's entire medical team practiced at the same hospital and we all had access to her medical records through a portal. I studied that MyChart app like there was going to be an exam later - I highly recommend having it.

Which leads me to another important item:

Medical Records & Permission

Get Permission Before You Need It.
One of the most loving, practical steps you can take is ensuring you have legal permission to access your loved one's medical information before a crisis occurs.
This may include:

- HIPAA authorization forms

- Being listed as a healthcare proxy

- Medical power of attorney

- Access to online patient portals

Permission to speak directly with doctors and care teams
Without this authorization, medical professionals may be legally unable to share information with you, even when you are the primary caregiver.
These conversations can feel uncomfortable.
Have them anyway.

Frame it as protection, not control:
"If there's ever an emergency, I want to be able to advocate for you the way you would want."

Getting permission early:

- reduces stress during emergencies

- prevents delays in care

- allows you to advocate confidently

- honors your loved one's wishes

This is not about taking over.

It's about being prepared.

Remember, preparation is empowerment.

Caregiver Guidance: Creating Rest in a Place That Never Sleeps

Everyone knows you don't get any real rest in the hospital. Between the beeping monitors, whirring machines, nurses doing their many jobs, food tray delivery and pickup, housekeeping, blood draws, doctor visits, multiple therapists, transportation shuttling patients to and from tests, IV changes, the bed alarm that goes off when you move the wrong way, that 4:00 a.m. blood draw, and the random staff member popping in looking for something — sleep is hard to come by.

I did what I could to make Mommy comfortable.
We had our silk pillowcases, good moisturizer, her tablet for puzzles, and her favorite hand lotion. There's only so much you can do when there are tubes, leads, and safety concerns, but I tried.
What was truly helpful — for both of us — was negotiating quiet time with her medical team.

Once they were satisfied that she was stable, they agreed not to disturb us between 11:00 p.m. and 5:00 a.m. The nurses monitored her vitals from their station, and we agreed to follow all safety protocols.

You can, within reason, make requests and tailor your loved one's care so it makes sense for them — not just the system.
The nurses did occasionally peek in quietly, but it never disturbed Mommy.

Of course, I slept with one eye open — because you probably know this already — as lethargic and immobile as our loved ones can be during the day, they often get energized and busy at night.

That's why honoring safety measures is essential.

Keep the bed rails up.

Make sure the alarm is on to alert you if they try to get up.

Use sleeves to cover IVs.

And yes — restraints, if necessary, though never without discussion and intention.

I can't tell you how many times I watched Mommy carefully maneuver herself to the edge of the bed, inch by inch, slide between the rails, and get one leg out before I asked her — from the dead silence —
"Where are you going?"

♡

Startled, she'd retreat and snap,

"Don't you ever sleep?"

No ma'am.

Not with Houdini Jr. for a roommate.

No sleep for me.

I was grateful I could call my big sister so we could laugh together about Mommy's nighttime escapades.

Sometimes laughter is the only thing that keeps you sane.

Caregiver Guidance: Navigating the Grief Before the Grief

When your loved one begins to decline - especially cognitively - you enter a kind of grief no one talks about.
It is real.
It is valid.
And it is one of the hardest parts of the caregiving journey.

Here are some gentle truths and tools to help you through it:

1. Understand: You Are Losing Them in Layers

Decline happens slowly.
Pieces of your parent slip away before anyone officially names it.

Every forgotten detail, every personality shift, every confusing interaction is a tiny loss - and tiny losses add up.

Your heart knows it before your mind does.

2. Release the Expectation That They Will "Be Themselves" Again

This is the hardest truth.

Some days they will feel like themselves.
Some days they won't.
And some days you'll see flashes - a comment, a smile, a familiar gesture -
that remind you of who they were.

Hold those moments.
But don't cling to the expectation that they'll return for good.

3. Don't Take Accusations or Outbursts Personally

They are not attacking you.
They are battling confusion, fear, and misfiring neurons.

What feels like betrayal is simply the illness speaking through them.

Repeat when needed:

"This is not my parent. This is the illness."

4. Allow Yourself to Feel What You Feel

You may feel sadness, anger, frustration, numbness, resentment, guilt, or despair.

Every emotion is normal.

There is no "right" way to grieve someone who is still alive.

5. Ask for Help - and Accept It

This cannot be said enough:

Ask for help.

Lean on family members and friends - yours and your loved one's. Tell people what you need. Let them show up for you.

And when people offer help?

Accept it.

You do not have to do it alone. You are not required to be a martyr.

Superwoman is a movie character, not a caregiving blueprint.

As my favorite social media licensed clinical psychologist, Dr. Raquel Martin says, "lose the cape!'

Your body and spirit need restoration.

Get a massage.
Take a nap.
Soak in the tub.
Step outside for air.
Eat a meal slowly.
Let someone else sit with your loved one while you rest.

You will be a better caregiver - clearer, calmer, stronger - if you allow yourself moments to breathe.

Please remember:

You don't have to do it alone.

6. Seek Professional Support Early

Therapists, grief counselors, social workers, and caregiver support groups can help you navigate:

- anticipatory grief
- overwhelm
- difficult emotions
- family dynamics
- decision-making

Getting help is not weakness.
It is wisdom.

7. Practice Emotional Detachment Without Losing Love

Detach from the behavior, not the person.
Detach from the illness, not the love.

This balance protects your heart while preserving your bond.

8. Make Space for Joy, Humor, and Light

There will still be moments of beauty:
- small jokes
- shared memories
- unexpected laughter
- gentle touch
- moments of clarity

Allow them.
They are medicine.

9. Give Yourself Permission to Grieve While They're Still Alive

This is not betrayal.
This is love in its rawest form.

You are grieving the slow, quiet loss of who they were
while still loving who they are now.

Your heart is stretched in impossible ways.
Be gentle with it.

Chapter Nine

When the Bottom Dropped Out

We were on the upswing after the second stroke.

Mommy was doing her exercises.
Taking her medications.
Eating well enough.
Getting stronger.

And then,
just when I thought we had found our rhythm again,
the bottom dropped out.

Mommy had been diagnosed in 2015 with CLL - Chronic
Lymphocytic Leukemia.
It had been in remission for years, quiet and well-behaved, tucked
away like an unwelcome guest who forgot they were invited.

But cancers have a way of remembering themselves.
And this one decided to rear its ugly head.

Suddenly, we were in and out of hospitals again.
Doctor after doctor.

Bloodwork, scans, new prescriptions, new fears.

Her medications increased.
Shots in her stomach at home.
Nurses and therapists in and out of the condo like a rotating cast
of characters.
IV bags, pill organizers, schedules, alarms, charts -
our life became a medical production with no intermission.

It seemed we had it under control.

Until we didn't.

The cancer morphed into another, more aggressive form.
It was bad.
And Mommy...
my fierce, stubborn, Southern Belle warrior...
began to give up.

She either stopped wanting to or being able to eat.
I couldn't make anything right anymore.
My sister, always more sensitive where our mother was concerned,
stopped trying to cook.
She couldn't take the rejection.
It cut too deep.

Even coffee, her favorite, became a battleground.

It was always bitter.

It turned into a running joke between my sister and me.
There we were, two grown women standing in front of our
mother like terrified contestants on a cooking show, holding our
breath as she lifted the cup to her lips.

She'd taste it -
pause -
and then grimace.

"Bitter."

We were crushed every time and still found a way to laugh through
the defeat.

If she didn't like one dish, I tossed it and made another.
Whatever she wanted, whatever she thought she could tolerate, we
tried to find it.

My ex-husband and his wife searched the entire city and
surrounding suburbs for anything she mentioned craving.
They were a blessing.

She tried her best to eat, but eventually, eating became an act of futility.
She could only manage a nutrition drink, and she resented that.
She would make her way to the dining room, shoulders squared with dignity, just to drink a bottle she didn't want.
You could see in her face how cruel it felt.

Her quality of life was slipping.
Her world was dimming.

We still went out when the weather permitted, but her eyesight was fading.
She couldn't see clearly, and I could feel her life slowly folding in on itself.

My heart was breaking.
She was slipping away, one quiet inch at a time.

Then she told me to send for her cousin in San Francisco — the cousin who was just a few years younger, the one she adored.

And that's when I knew.

The end was near.

A few months after her previous birthday, I had asked her how long she wanted to live.

She answered, matter-of-fact,
"Until the age of 87."

She said it like a weather report, like a tax filing deadline, like a fact already carved in stone.

We celebrated her 87th birthday on April 20th.

We sang.
She danced - just a little sway, but it was enough.
I baked a cake.
She tasted it.
We smiled through our fear.

And I held my breath every day after that.

Watching.
Waiting.
Listening to the subtle shifts.
Feeling her spirit preparing to leave.

♡

Less than a month later,
she was gone.

♡

Part III ~ Understanding Death While Living

Chapter Ten

Understanding Death Through the Lens of Life

It was 2015.

I was at dinner in Negril, Jamaica, when the news broke that legendary singer Natalie Cole had died.

Around the table came a chorus of,

"Oh no... I can't believe it."

My mother's cousin from San Francisco leaned forward and said, almost casually,

"I don't know why we say that when someone dies.

This ain't no permanent gig."

The table grew quiet.

But her words echoed inside me long after the plates were cleared.

This life - this earthly, physical, breathing life - is not permanent.

That part we know.

But we rarely say it aloud.

We move through life as if we are guaranteed a certain amount of time, as if the people we love are fixtures instead of miracles.

Something shifted in me after that dinner.

I began exploring death from every angle I could:

Spiritually.
Scientifically.
Emotionally.
Energetically.

What was death, really?

What was transition?
What did it mean for the soul?

And maybe more importantly...
What did it produce?

The Garden's Answer

As a gardener, I already knew the answer.
I had always known it.

Death produces new life.
Always.
Without fail.

A seed must die - literally break apart, surrender its shape, dissolve
its outer shell - before anything living can emerge from it.

A seed cannot become what it's meant to be
until it ceases to be what it currently is.

Every flower in my garden had once been a funeral of sorts.
Every herb, every leaf, every blossom had died first.
Death is a beginning, not an end.

So why wouldn't the same be true for us?

The Butterfly's Truth

I also raise butterflies; Monarchs and Swallowtails.
I have witnessed transitions so sacred, so impossible, they feel like
scripture.

The caterpillar doesn't just transform.
It liquefies.

Inside the chrysalis, it dissolves into something unrecognizable.
It becomes a formless soup before reorganizing itself into a new
creature with wings.

Let me say that again:

It becomes nothing
before it becomes everything.

If you cut open the chrysalis too soon,
you won't find a half-formed butterfly.
You'll find liquid.

Pure potential.
No shape.
No identity.

No future yet revealed.

If that's not death and resurrection,
what is?

So as I watched my mother decline,
as I watched pieces of her slip away,
as I grieved the woman I knew even before she took her last breath,

I held onto this truth:

Death is not an ending.
It is a releasing.
A dissolving.
A returning.
A becoming.

My mother was shedding one form
to take another.

Just like the seed.
Just like the butterfly.
Just like everything God made.

♡

Her body was not her limit.
Her humanity was not her final shape.
Her transition was not a disappearance.

It was a metamorphosis.

Dear Mommy,

I feel so helpless.
So useless.
Because I can't fix this.

Whatever is happening, whatever is taking you away from me, I can't stop it.

And the hardest part is knowing...

I'm not meant to stop it.

I have to surrender to what is.
I have to embrace what's to come, even when it breaks me.

My only goal now is simple:
to keep you comfortable,
to keep you safe,
and to spend as much time with you as possible.

Ooh - I know.
We'll go get manicures!
That always makes us feel better.

It's a small thing but a sacred thing - the ritual of care, the soft touch, the moment of normal.

Your cousin will be here soon.
I'm bracing myself to give you your time alone together - time to talk, to laugh, to cry, to say whatever your spirit needs to say before your departure.

You've outlived all your siblings, many of your elders, and quite a few of your closest friends.
And I can sense... you're ready to go.

I'm trying to prepare myself for that truth, even though every part of me wishes I could hold you here forever.

I know I've been snappy lately - I told you that when I apologized.

Please know:
I am never angry with you.
I'm angry with the diseases.
I'm angry with what they're doing to you.
I pray you understand the difference.

♡

Mommy, I'm right here.
I'm not going anywhere.
We'll walk this next stretch together, hand in hand, just like
always.

xoxoxo
Robin

Chapter Eleven

The Womb and the Transition

You may have heard this analogy before,
but in case you haven't...

Imagine you're in the womb.

It's dark.
It's warm.
It's wet.

All the nourishment you need is provided effortlessly through the
umbilical cord.
You want for nothing.
You float in total peace.
This is your world.
This is your life.
This is all you know.

Then suddenly,
everything changes.

The walls start closing in around you.

There is squeezing, pressure, pushing.
Your safe, warm universe is collapsing, and you don't understand why.

You're being forced out of the only existence you've ever known.

You are pushed into a narrow canal.
There is light, bright, unforgiving light.

There are strange voices, a woman screaming - nothing like the soft familiar sounds that have comforted you for months.
Cold, metallic instruments may tug at your body.
Hands pull you forward.

You resist, but resistance doesn't save you.
You are moving whether you want to or not.

And if you had the consciousness to think it,
you would probably believe you were dying.

Because everything familiar is ending.
Your world is collapsing.
Your environment is gone.
Your identity as you know it is dissolving.
This must be the end of your life.

But it isn't.

It's the beginning.

It's the beginning of life outside the womb -
a world bigger, brighter, more expansive than anything you could
have imagined from inside the darkness.

A world you were always meant to enter.

A world you couldn't understand until you got there.

That is how I feel about death.

Death is the squeezing,
the narrowing,
the bright unfamiliar light,
the strange voices,
the letting go of the only world we know.

It feels like the end.

But it is just the beginning of a new phase -
one more expansive, more luminous, more liberating than
anything we can comprehend from inside this human experience.

Just as birth is a transition from one existence to another,
so is death.

It is not a disappearance.
It is an emergence.
A continuation.
A return.
A remembering.

And that's what I believe.
With my whole heart.
And I want to give Death a new, purposeful and joyous meaning.

♡

Part IV ~ The Threshold

Chapter Twelve

The Day Everything Shifted

I gathered the courage to speak to someone about hospice.

Not because I was giving up - far from it.
But because I wanted to understand our options.
I wanted to know what "comfort care" really meant.
I wanted to know how to protect my mother from the trauma of
constant emergency room visits.

They reassured me that people sometimes come out of hospice.
That hospice isn't always the end.
That sometimes it is simply a sacred pause -
a chance for the body to rest and the soul to decide.

But really, I just wanted what was best for Mommy.
And the back-and-forth between home and the ER?
That wasn't it.

We had been in and out of the hospital for months.
Dehydration.
Pain.
Weakness.
Fatigue.

Each visit took more out of her than the last.

She didn't want to go anymore - and honestly, I didn't blame her.

Hospitals can help with healing, but they can also break the spirit of a person already fighting too many battles.

Then one morning in May, everything changed.

I sensed something was wrong at the condo.

A heaviness.

A tug in my chest.

A knowing.

I called.

No answer.

I activated the cameras.

I couldn't see her - but I could hear her cousin in the background repeating the F-word over and over.

I spoke through the camera, voice shaking,
"What's going on?"

Her cousin answered that Mommy was stuck in the bathtub.

Stuck.

I called my younger brother, who lived in the same building.
And by the grace of God, he was home - something rare.

He raced upstairs, and when he got there,
he unleashed his own string of F-words,
which told me everything I needed to know.

Mommy was somehow wedged in her bathtub in a way no one
could explain.
Not even her.

My brother lifted her out, carried her gently, put her in bed, and
held the nutrition drink while she sipped it through a straw.
He FaceTimed me and said he would stay with her until her
caregiver - our true earth angel - arrived.

Meanwhile, I was dealing with a plumbing issue at my house,
waiting for the plumber to show up.
Life doesn't pause for grief, or fear, or emergencies.
It continues, indifferent to your struggle.

The caregiver arrived and told me everything was okay.
"Take your time," she said.

But thirty minutes later, she called again.

Her tone was different.
Urgent.
Steady.

"Come now."

I left the plumber in the house with the door open.

When I arrived, the caregiver explained that Mommy still had the
Ensure from that morning in her mouth.
She hadn't swallowed it.

I tried to give her water.
She couldn't drink it.
The swallow reflex simply wasn't there.

I asked,
"Mommy, can I take you to the ER?"

She said yes.

I told her,
"We'll get you some fluids and come back home."

But what I didn't know - what I learned later -
is that when the organs begin shutting down,

the body knows.

The body is brilliant.
It refuses food and water when it can no longer process them.
It stops asking for what it cannot use.

We were in the ER waiting room when her angel - the caregiver
who loved her like blood - walked in to be with us.
We were never alone.
TMH made sure of that.

Once we were taken back and settled, the doctors explained what
was happening inside her body.
They told me they could not release her.
She was too fragile.
Too far along.

I turned to Mommy and asked the only question that mattered,
"Are you okay with staying?"

She whispered softly,
"Yes."

If she'd said no, we would have gone home.
No debate.
She was the boss.
Always.

She was freezing.
I didn't have our go bags.
So, we got her warm and toasty and her angel stayed while I ran
home to get them.

I stopped in the doorway and asked,
"Are you sure you're okay with me leaving?"

She responded with her famous one-word reassurance,
"Positive."

And I believed her.

But the moment I got in the car...
I broke.

The kind of break that comes from the deepest part of the soul.
The kind of break that says,
This is it. Things will not be the same when I return.

I sobbed the entire drive home.
The kind of sob you feel in your bones.
The kind that sounds like a surrender.

Because somewhere inside,
I knew we had crossed the threshold.

There is a before.
There is an after.
And this was the line between them.

Chapter Thirteen

The Last Days

They were just taking her up to her room by the time I got back.
I begged the angel — her caregiver who had already gone above
and beyond — to go home and rest.
She had done more than enough.

On my drive back from the house, I called the nice hospice lady.
We scheduled an appointment for Monday morning.
It was Friday.

Mommy wasn't talking much anymore.
She drifted in and out of sleep, mostly resting.

I called her oncologist.
He was stunned.

"I just saw her last Friday!" he said, disbelief thick in his voice.
"What could have happened?"

When I mentioned that I had called hospice, he said,
"Hospice? I'm coming to the hospital to see her myself."

They had formed a bond - a real one - and he had held onto hope for her recovery.

When I told Mommy he was coming, she perked up, just a little. A faint smile crossed her face.

"She doesn't believe he'd come," I whispered to myself.

"You matter," I reminded her softly.

It was late Friday night.
We went to sleep.

By Saturday morning, she wasn't talking at all.
Her responsiveness was limited — and only to me.

Most of her grandchildren FaceTimed her;
a few couldn't bear to see her in that state.
The great-grands left messages.

I reached out to some of her closest friends so they could speak to her one last time.

I played the video birthday card we'd made for her during covid - so many people, so many faces, so much love poured into those recorded messages.

She smiled.

The nurses moved in and out, busy with weekend rhythms.
Physical therapy stopped by - I shooed them away.
This wasn't the time.
Business as usual didn't apply anymore.

By Saturday afternoon, her condition declined rapidly.
She wasn't speaking at all and responded only to my presence.

Hospice arrived, and we set things up for her return home -
Tuesday morning at 10 a.m.

Her oncologist kept his word.
When he walked in and saw her,
he audibly gasped.
He lost his composure - truly lost it - and had to rush out of the room.

When he returned, eyes red, he said quietly,

"The cancer has reached her brain."

♡

He spoke to her softly, gently -
as a doctor,
a friend,
a man who cared.

Her angel caregiver showed up at the hospital on her off day.
She brought food and sat with me.
I hadn't eaten since early Friday afternoon.
I didn't even realize how empty I was until she placed the
container in my hands.

By Sunday, Mommy wasn't trying to speak anymore.
We spent quiet time together -
just presence, just breath.

Her cousin came by and spent the night with us.
We cackled - truly cackled - the way only our family can.
That laughter held us like a hammock, keeping us from collapsing
under the weight of what was coming.

I had begun sleeping in the bed with Mommy.
Her cousin curled up on the hospital couch-bed, the sterile room
had become a sacred space.

On Monday, Mommy began tugging at her IVs.
I asked gently,
"Mommy, do you want them out?"

She nodded, yes.

I called my sister.

She had an important doctor's appointment on Tuesday - the
whole reason she had gone back to Alabama.
She'd already booked a flight back for Friday.

I asked Mommy,
"Will you wait for her until Friday?"

She shook her head no.

My sister moved her flight up to Tuesday right after her
appointment.

I told her what Mommy wanted -
to stop all life support and just ride it out.

She said she trusted me to make the right decision.

I told the nurses to remove everything.
They left one low-dose sedative line in place,
"just in case she becomes agitated," they said.

I nodded.
We agreed.

I was scared beyond comprehension.

I kneeled at Mommy's bedside
and the sobs ripped their way out of me.

Deep, wrenching sobs -
the kind that come from the marrow, not the lungs.

Mommy grew agitated, thrashing slightly.
She felt my fear.

I stood quickly, wiped my face, steadied my breath,
and whispered,

"I'm sorry. I'm okay. I'm right here."

She calmed instantly.
Peace washed over her.

I realized then:
I had to be her peace.
Not her fear.
Not her anguish.
Her peace.

I climbed back into bed beside her,
wrapped my arm around her,
and we took a nap.

Just like mothers and daughters do.

Just like we had done
my entire life.

Chapter Fourteen

Riding Out on a Moonbeam

Being able to hold you in my arms as we shared the last few
moments of your breath
was one of the most profound moments of my life.

It reminded me of bringing my three sons into the world -
as though I was helping birth you into your next mission.

That day felt magical.
Otherworldly.

A rainbow appeared in the center of the three large windows in
our hospital room.
I whispered,
"Mommy... is this your ride?"

You didn't respond.

Later, a giant, fluffy cloud with what looked like a doorway at its
center drifted by.

I asked again,
"Mommy... is this your ride?"

But it wasn't.

I spent that day tending to you the way you tended to me my
whole life.
Braiding your hair.
Talking to you.
Rubbing your feet.
Anointing your body with rose, frankincense, and myrrh.

I told you how brave you were.
What an amazing mother you'd been.
How deeply, endlessly, eternally I love you.

The moon that night was beautiful—round, bright, and looking
full.
We lay in silence for a while, soft meditation music playing in the
background.
After a time, I sensed you wanted quiet.
I turned the music off,
and we rested in absolute stillness.

Our nurse slipped out without a sound, whispering that she
would watch you from her station.
She truly was a godsend.

We slept peacefully together until you stirred, just after 2:00
a.m.
The time for stillness had passed.
I put on our favorite meditation playlist.

I could see the moon through the left window - high, full,
glowing like it was keeping vigil.
Your eyes were still closed, relaxed and peaceful, just as they had
been all day.

We lay together in the bed, your head resting on my chest.
Our breath moved as one:

You'd exhale -
I'd inhale.

I'd exhale -
you'd inhale.

A perfect harmony.
A perfect goodbye.

All day I'd been begging you to open your beautiful eyes one more time.
I wanted to look into them and say
I love you.

And selfishly...
I wanted one last selfie.
I already had so many, but I needed one more.

As the moon moved to the center of the three windows,
I heard the nurse slip quietly back into the room.

Just then, your eyes fluttered open.

My heart soared.

I told you everything I needed to say.
All of it.
Every word.

I almost forgot the photo,
but you indulged me one final time.

Your eyes slowly closed again.
I couldn't be more grateful.

It was 2:40 a.m.
We continued to breathe.

As your breathing slowed,
the nurse gave me a silent signal.

We continued to breathe -
slower, deeper, slower still.

I turned my head slightly to the left, trying to keep the tears from
falling onto your face,
they had agitated you earlier.

And that's when I saw the moon.

Front and center in the window.
Full.
Waiting.

"Mommy... is this your ride?"
I whispered.

We continued to breathe.

♡

At 3:00 a.m.,
we shared your final breath.

Ron Yuval's - Wood, played softly in the background.
The moon stood witness.

And just like that—
you rode out on a moonbeam,
with the stars lighting your path.

The full moon has never been the same for me since.

Dear Mommy - "Walking You to the Door"

Dear Mommy,

I fully expected us to leave the hospital together, the way we always did.

Hospice had already prepared everything at home. The special bed was set up, the equipment was in place, and they were scheduled to pick you up at 10:15 a.m. I thought we had a plan. I thought we were going home.

But you had other plans.

You let me know you wanted the IVs removed. We agreed to keep only the low-dose pain medication, just in case, but you didn't want to be drugged or drowsy. You didn't want to miss anything. You didn't want to leave anything unsaid. And I didn't want you to be in pain.

There was no denying it anymore - the end of your life here, on this plane, was coming.

So I made sure to tell you everything I needed to say.

I thanked you for being the best mother I could have ever asked for.
I told you how much I loved you.
I made sure you were comfortable and felt safe.

I didn't want regrets.
Yes, I had a few maybe I should have thoughts,
but none big enough to disturb the peace we had created in that sacred space.

It was you and me.
Just like always.

Your little worry wrinkle appeared - the one you've had all my life, right above your nose. I smoothed it out with my thumb and whispered:

"I'm right here.
No need to be afraid.
I'll stay with you to the very end.
I'll walk you to the door...
but I won't go in with you.
It's not my time."

Mommy, it felt like the very first day of school -
when the parent walks the child to the door, heart full of
excitement and fear.
You stand there, knowing you can't go inside with them.
You have to trust.
You have to believe.

Except this time, the roles were reversed.
I was the one handing you off to your next adventure.

There could have been seven people in the room.
It still would have been only us.
Mommy and me.

And sometimes I marvel -
How did I not lose my mind?

How did I not fall apart?
How did I hold my best friend, my mother, in my arms in the
final hours of her life?

I know now:

I became fully present.

I focused on your breath.
I focused on mine.
Slowly, quietly, our breathing synchronized.

Mommy, your breath was the first music I ever heard
and the last blessing you ever gave me.

Your first breath carried hope.
Your final breath carried release.
And everything in between was sacred love -
a lifetime of it -
carried on the invisible river flowing between us.

The breath is sacred.

Breath is the bridge between two worlds.
When we enter, we inhale.
When we exit, we exhale.

Breath is spirit made visible.
Breath is presence, love, memory, grief, surrender, and soul.
The breath is the ancestors moving through us.

I took a deep breath for both of us.
Held it.
Released it.

And then, when the moment came...
Mommy, I inhaled your last exhale
and held it
as long
as I possibly
could.

I will carry that breath,
your final blessing,
for the rest of my life.

xoxoxo,
Robin

Chapter Fifteen

The Last Acts of Love

The nurse had silently slipped back into the room.
She stood there watching me hold Mommy so gently,
as if afraid to break the magical spell surrounding us.
And truly,
that moment was magical.

I had ushered Mommy right up to the door of her transition.
I made it clear, spirit to spirit, that I couldn't walk inside with her -
but I would be beside her all the way to the threshold.

She was timid at first.
There was a tiny crease between her brows, that familiar
questioning look she always got when entering something
unfamiliar.

But as I massaged her forehead and whispered,
"Don't be afraid. I'm here with you,"
her spirit steadied.
She strengthened her resolve.
She faced the unknown with curiosity and purpose,
just as she had faced every major moment of her life.

The nurse finally spoke, softly apologetic.
She told me she had to get a doctor to verify the time of death,
and she slipped out, leaving Mommy and me alone in the
hospital bed.

A few minutes later, the doctor rounded the corner.
As he pulled the curtain back, I sat upright.

I am convinced he had to change his pants after leaving that
room.
I more than startled him.

I couldn't appreciate the humor in that moment,
but later -
oh, I laughed until I cried.

He and the sweet nurse explained that he needed to perform a
few standard checks.
They stood there awkwardly, shuffling in place, until it dawned
on me:

They needed me to get out of the bed.

They were too polite,
or too nervous,
to say it.

I called my sisters.
I called my dad.
I sent individual texts to family and close friends.

I also reached out by text to someone dear to me who is a funeral
director, asking for recommendations.
She immediately called me back.

"This is not a text conversation," she said gently.
It was 4:00 a.m.

She took care of me.
She directed me to the best person she knew.
And he handled Mommy, and my family, with profound care.

The nurse reentered the room.
She told me she needed to wash Mommy's body to prepare her for
the morgue.

I asked if I could help her.

She stared at me for a long moment, as though measuring
something sacred between us.
Then she nodded.
I promised I would follow her lead.

Together, we gently washed Mommy's body.
I prayed as I swabbed her skin, mirroring every move the nurse made.
When she paused, I paused.
We lifted and turned Mommy in perfect unison, communicating through silent gestures—
like dance partners.

Mommy's body became heavy and stiff quickly—
the speed of it surprised me—
we worked together with grace.

When we finished, we sat on the couch for a few quiet minutes.

There were tears shining in the nurse's eyes.

She told me her mother had fallen ill a few years earlier.
Her grandparents, not wanting to disturb her, took her mom to a different hospital—the one she didn't work in.
They thought they were sparing her stress.

But her mother passed away before she could get there.

She had never gotten to be with her.
Never held her.
Never washed her.

Never said goodbye.

As tears rolled down both our faces,
she explained that each time she paused while washing Mommy,
she prayed. She communed with her mother.

That final act—
washing Mommy's body together in that sacred silence—
healed a wound she had carried for years.

I couldn't help but marvel.

Even in death,
Mommy was giving.
Mommy was healing.
Mommy was ministering without speaking a word.

We embraced before she left the room.
She reminded me that I had until 9:00 a.m. to say my goodbyes.

♡

Later, when I asked for her by name so I could thank her again, no one knew who I was talking about.

Not one person recognized my description.
No one knew who she was.

I wasn't the least bit surprised.

It was a supernatural day.

Chapter Sixteen

The Longest Walk

I waited until about 9:10 - maybe 9:15 - before walking to the nurses' station to ask where the morgue personnel were.
I stood there expecting a simple, procedural answer.

Instead, every nurse behind that desk looked at me as if I had two heads.

One of the younger nurses walked around the counter and pulled me gently to the side.
With the softest voice, she said,

"They're waiting for you to leave."

I stared at her, stunned.

I told her, in no uncertain terms,
"There's no way I'm leaving my mother like that.
Naked.
Alone.
Exposed to the world."

She shook her head firmly.

"No.

There is no way we would put her in a body bag and zip it up, in front of you.

Trust me, we've done this a thousand times.

You do not want to see that."

Up until that moment, I had been a pillar of strength.

I had made the calls.

Handled the arrangements.

Cancelled hospice.

Scheduled the pickup of all the equipment they had set up at the house.

Reached out to her closest friends.

Made list after list after list:

- Call the lawyer
- Contact her medical support team
- Handle the bank
- Pay outstanding bills
- Put her car in storage
- Notify the necessary agencies

There were so many things to do.

I spoke to Mommy the whole time, out loud, letting her know I had it under control.

But now...
now we had a problem.

We had a ritual.

Whenever Mommy was discharged,
I would help her get dressed and ready to go.
Then I would go retrieve the car and pull around to the patient pick-up area,
and a nurse would bring her down to me.

That was our rhythm.
Our normal.

But today, that wasn't happening.

I wasn't bringing her home.
I wasn't meeting her at the door.
I wasn't helping her into the car.

I was leaving Mommy behind.

♡

Abandoning her in her most vulnerable state.

My body understood before my mind did.

I entered the elevator and the door closed.
And in that tiny metal box, the truth hit me.

I slid down the wall,
and a sound came out of me that did not feel human.

A primal scream,
torn from a depth I didn't know existed.

The kind of sound that only comes when the soul breaks.

Grief erupted through me,
violent, uncontrollable,
a motherless child in an elevator.

I felt awful.
Empty.
Like I had failed her.

Even though I had done everything right,
even though I had held her through her last breath,
protected her dignity,
washed her body with my own hands -
this moment felt like betrayal.

Walking away from her was the hardest moment of my life.

Part V ~ The World After

Chapter Seventeen

When the World Reaches Out

Logically, I knew I wasn't abandoning my mother.

I knew her spirit - her essence, her real self - had left her avatar
hours earlier.
That moment was the holiest of my life.
I was there.
I witnessed it.
I felt the air change.
I felt the veil open.
I knew she was gone.

But my heart and brain hadn't reconciled.
My human self hadn't caught up with my spiritual understanding.

I felt like the worst daughter in the world.
How would my sister forgive me?
How would I forgive me?

The drive home felt eternal.

♡

When I finally reached the house, my youngest son was there
waiting—
open arms, steady shoulder, warm breakfast waiting for me on the
stove.
It was the worst day of my life,
but I was held.

Even Coco Chanel knew something was wrong.
She stayed close, followed me from room to room, eyes full of
concern.

Naturally, the calls and texts started coming in.
People meant well -
I knew they did -
but grief is a sacred, tender moment.
Not everyone knows how to enter that space with care.

So let's normalize something:

Allowing people to handle grief with grace, space, and choice.

And let's talk about what to say
- and what not to say -
when someone loses a loved one.

Because words matter.
Presence matters.
Silence matters.
Tone matters.
Timing matters.

Having been on both sides of the conversation, and not knowing what to say that's sincerely helpful, I'd like to offer some suggestions from my observations.
Here's a few examples that were comforting to me and that I could embrace saying as well - I struggle with what to say too.
1. "I'm so sorry for your loss."

Simple. Gentle. Human.
No fixing. No explaining. Just presence.

2. "I'm here for you if you want company or if you want space."

Offer choice.
Grief needs room to breathe.

3. "How can I support you today?"

Not "Let me know if you need anything."
The grieving person cannot think that far ahead.
Give them something solid and immediate.

4. "Your loved one was..."

Share a memory (be mindful and discerning).
A story.
A moment.
Grievers cling to every word that proves their loved one mattered.

5. "I love you."

Don't underestimate how grounding that can be.

6. Silence.

Sometimes silence is the kindest language.
Sitting beside someone without filling space is an act of deep respect.

On the other hand, these fell flat and honestly, were irritating. That's not what anyone is trying to be, it's typically something we heard along the way and thought it was the right thing to say.

1. "They're in a better place."

Even if true, it doesn't soothe fresh grief.
It dismisses the pain of missing them here.

2. "God doesn't give you more than you can handle."

This implies the griever should be strong instead of held.
It spiritualizes suffering rather than comforting it.

3. "I know exactly how you feel."

No, you don't.
Grief is personal, even when circumstances are similar.

4. "At least they lived a long life."

"Long" is irrelevant when you love someone.
Loss hurts at 17 or 87.

5. "Be strong."

For who?
For what?
Strength is not required in grief - truth is.

6. "Everything happens for a reason."

Not now.
Not ever in the beginning.

7. Unsolicited stories about other people's deaths.

This is not the moment to compare losses, trauma, or tragedies.

As far as what you can DO, I'm guilty of asking - what can I do? - here's a few offerings that genuinely felt supportive:

1. Bring food (without hovering).

Grief steals appetite and energy.
Drop it off. Don't linger unless invited.

2. Offer specific acts of service:

- "I'm going to the store. Can I pick up basics for you?"
- "Can I walk the dog?"
- "Can I handle x, y, or z for today?"

Specificity helps.

3. Check in weeks later.

After the funeral, people disappear.
But grief grows louder in the quiet.

4. Say their loved one's name.

The grieving want to know their person lives on in memory.

5. Respect boundaries.

Let them not answer the phone.
Let them not respond to texts.
Let them grieve in their own rhythm.

Grief has no calendar.
No finish line.
No "shoulds."

And last, but not least - now is not the time to share their loved ones secrets. Please, honor their wishes and honor your word.

If they're a hugger, a quiet hug goes a long way.

I knew that people were expressing their love the best way they knew how and that people say what they think is comforting and might comfort others. I extended grace and will continue to do so.

Chapter Eighteen

The Sign

I know I told you I asked Mommy for one last thing -
to open her eyes.

And she did.
My girl.
My champion.
My mother who never left me hanging, even at the threshold of
eternity.

But I asked her for something else, too.

Because I don't believe that death - as we know it - is our final
destination,
I asked her for a sign.

Nothing dramatic.
No ghostly apparition like the Spirits in A Christmas Carol.
No face on toast or misty silhouette floating by silk curtains at
dawn.

I wanted something specific.

Something particular to us.
Something I would recognize instantly.

As you know by now, I called my mother every morning.
Every morning.
No matter where I was -
Chicago, Atlanta, Jamaica -
I greeted my day with "Good morning, Mommy."

For decades.

But now...
what was I supposed to do
tomorrow?

I woke up early the next morning to write a love letter to my father.
He wasn't doing well.
Even after decades apart, he still loved Mommy deeply,
and I wanted - if I could - to lift his spirits.

As I wrote, Coco Chanel suddenly began barking at the back door.
It was too early for her to go out,
but she was aging, and I thought,
She must need to relieve herself, regardless of the time.

I was still in bed,
still dreading facing a day without Mommy,
still trying to figure out how to breathe in this new world.

By the time I made my way to the kitchen,
Coco was beside herself.
I hurried so she wouldn't have an accident.

I swung the doors open -
but instead of running out, she stepped back
and looked at me.

I stood there confused.
I coaxed her.
She refused.

Just as I was closing the door,
something caught my eye.

In my garden -
in my glorious rose bush -
was the tiniest hummingbird I had ever seen.
A baby.
Still shimmering.
Still new to the world.

I threw my head back and laughed,
joy bursting through grief like sunlight cracking open a storm.

"Good morning, Mommy," I said, smiling.

Of course she sent a hummingbird.
The one creature whose wings move so fast
you can't see them -
only feel the vibration.
Just like spirit.
Just like her.

That was her sign.
Precise.
Perfect.
Undeniable.
Ours.

And oh, it was the sweetest hello.

Reflection: The Meaning of Hummingbirds

Hummingbirds have carried spiritual meaning across cultures for thousands of years. They are tiny, delicate creatures - yet fierce, powerful, and impossibly brave. Their wings beat so rapidly they blur into invisibility, creating a hum that feels like spirit in motion. Their presence often arrives like a whisper from another world.

It makes sense to me that Mommy would choose a hummingbird.

Especially because hummingbirds were our thing.

I have several hummingbird feeders in my garden, along with flowers planted just for them. Mommy and I would spend hours watching them dance in and out of the blooms. She was mesmerized that I had hummingbirds in the middle of the city - zipping, hovering, sipping nectar as if they'd discovered a hidden sanctuary among concrete and skyline.

We shared so many quiet moments like that,
just watching them hover and glitter in the air.
It was our meditation.
Our ritual.
Our joy.

♡

So when a hummingbird appeared the morning after she
transitioned -
a tiny baby, shimmering in my rose bush -
it wasn't random.

It was familiar.
It was intimate.
It was ours.

Across ancestral traditions and folklore, hummingbirds often
symbolize:

Visitations from loved ones who have passed

Many cultures believe hummingbirds carry messages between
worlds.
Their sudden appearance often means:
"I'm here. I'm with you. I'm okay."

For us, it meant:
"Good morning, Robin."

Joy in the midst of sorrow.

Hummingbirds defy gravity.
They hover where others fall.
They bring color to the darkest spaces.

They remind us that even in grief,
Joy can pierce the clouds.

Resilience and endurance

Despite their size, hummingbirds migrate astonishing distances.
They survive storms mid-air.
They rest on nothing but faith and instinct.

They teach us that the heart, too, can survive impossible distances -
between presence and absence,
between a life lived together
and a life we must now navigate alone.

The bridge between worlds

Their wings beat up to 80 times per second -
too fast to see,
only fast enough to feel.

♡

The line between visible and invisible dissolves.

A hummingbird is more vibration than bird,
more frequency than form,
more message than creature.

Love that revisits us

Some believe hummingbirds appear when the heart is broken
and someone you love is trying to help piece it back together.

They arrive exactly when needed.
Exactly where needed.
Exactly how needed.

Mommy knew that.
She knew a hummingbird would be specific to us.
Instantly recognizable.
Undeniable.
A perfect hello from the other side.

The baby hummingbird in my rose bush
wasn't just a sign.

♡

It was continuity.

It was love choosing a new doorway.

And it was only the beginning.

Dear Mommy,

It's been three years since you left us, riding out on that full moon into the ether.

I still think of you every day.
I can't say it's gotten easier.
What has happened is that I've grown more grateful—for the time we had, for every memory, for every lesson. They've all become more precious.

I still miss your physical touch.
I miss being able to call you at any time, knowing you'd make everything better—sometimes with just a few words, sometimes with no words at all.

To be honest, the thought of not missing you is unimaginable.
It isn't even something I want.

I don't ever want to stop missing you.
I believe that if I woke up one day and didn't miss you, it would break me.
What a cruel world that would be.

I still wake up and say, "Good morning, Mommy."
Sometimes I say it out loud.
Sometimes I whisper it only in my thoughts.

But when I begin my day that way, I'm guaranteed it's going to
be an adventure.

In some ways, you're even more present than before.
You're literally everywhere.

Mommy, a few weeks after the hummingbird sighting, something
else happened.
The twelve swallowtail chrysalises that had overwintered began to
emerge - one after another. Sometimes two in a single day. At
least one every day. It was absolutely breathtaking.

I remember saying, "Oh wow, Mom... look at you."

You were so eager to show me transformation.
So many lessons.
So much beauty.

You were my first teacher, and you continue to teach me from
beyond the veil.

I'm learning now that death is expansion - not finality.
Death has gotten such a bad reputation.

I'm paying attention, Mommy.
I see you.
I hear you.
All the time.

You used to ask me why I went to all the trouble to do this or that.
And I always answered,
"Because one day, one of us won't be here. And I don't want the
other to have regrets."

You were - and continue to be - the best.

Thank you for loving me so thoroughly.

xoxoxo,
Robin

Chapter Nineteen

Good morning Mommy!

Epilogue

Because She Lived

April 20, 2025

Today is Mommy's Birthday

To this day, my Mommy has lived inside my heart for 64 years.

She has been my role model and my champion for longer than that.

My mother nurtured me, loved me, and dreamed of me even before I was born - while she herself was growing inside her mother's womb.

I was there with her, in spirit, even then.

And I have loved her ever since.

I am the woman I am today because of my amazing mother.

I am alive today because of my amazing mother.

You say she is dead.

I say, without hesitation, you are mistaken.

My mother is not dead.

She lives in me.

She lives in my sister.

She lives in our children, and their children too.

She lives in the hearts and minds of those she loved - and those who loved her.

She lives in the glint of my eye,

the sway of my hips,

and the melody of my laughter.

Because she lived, I live.

Because I live, she lives.

She is alive.

I adore my mother - and I make no secret of it.

If you know me, you know my mother.

If you know my mother, you know me.

It's a beautiful thing:

Mommy and me.

Me and Mommy.

Always Mommy and me.

It will always be Mommy and me.

Each morning when I rise to meet the new day, I say her name with joy.

I sing, Good morning, Mommy! - just as I have, day after day, year after year.

It remains a highlight of every day:

Good Morning, Mommy!

I say her name.

♡

I say her name.

Say her name, say her name:

Her name is Rosa.

The name Rosa means "rose."

The rose is a flower that has been associated with love, beauty, and passion throughout history.

It's no surprise, then, that the name Rosa is often given to girls seen as beautiful, loving, graceful, gentle, and passionate.

The name Rosa carries an elegance and sophistication that is impossible to ignore.

A beautiful name for my beautiful mother.

Today is her birthday, and today I celebrate.

It is a day to celebrate the 87 years my mother, Rosa, graced this earthly atmosphere — plus the three years beyond.

♡

It is right and just to celebrate her life with thanksgiving and praise:

Because she lived, because we live, she lives.

So today, April 20th, 2025, I shout,

"Good Morning, Happy Birthday, Mommy!"
just as I always have - since I knew how - since I was part of Team Mommy and Me.

Happy Birthday, Mommy!

(Disclaimer: In reality, it's Mommy, Bonnie (my older sister - the favorite), and then me. But in MY poem (and maybe sometimes my mind, I'm in therapy, we listen and we don't judge), it's Mommy and me! And that's my business.)

The Ring Between Us

Mommy and I had a ritual. When we arrived for our hospital stays, she would take her onyx ring off her finger, hand it to me, and I would put it on one of mine.

When it was time to go home, we would reverse the process. That final weekend, I asked mommy where she got this beautiful, ornate silver ring with its shiny black stone.

Mommy was always fashionable, we shopped at the best stores on Michigan Avenue and State Street, for as long I could remember. I loved our visits to CD Peacock, one of her favorite jewelry stores, where she'd find something elegant and unique. She was whispering at this point, so I had to lean in close to hear her.

"I" she swallowed and cleared her throat. "I, em, em, I" - she was struggling to get it out. I found myself holding my breath as I leaned in closer. "I found it on the ground in front of the house."

Once I picked my jaw off the floor, I laughed until my side hurt. I chuckle every time I put her ring on my finger now. That weekend broke the circle of our ritual, her ring sealed the infinite essence of our love.

Pictured in this photo:

My mother, my sister, and I, highlighting the beaded bracelets my sister's granddaughter made for us. Of course, mommy's treasured onyx ring.

About the Author

Robin E Anderson - is a mother, grandmother, sister, writer, caregiver, gardener, photographer, and spiritual practitioner whose work explores grief, legacy, and the sacred work of loving through transition. Drawing from lived experience as her mother's primary caregiver, Robin weaves memoir, ritual, and practical wisdom to guide others through loss with honesty, reverence, and grace. When Our Mothers Become Ancestors is her first book.